Tech Tips

for the

Tech-Timid

Tech Tips for the Tech-Timid

Sue Wilhite

Ms Tech Coach

Positively Success Publishing
Rohnert Park, California

Cover Art: © Depositphotos: fotopitu (Josep M Rovirosa Fortuny)

ISBN 13: 978-0-9985099-5-2

First Printing: June 2023

Printed in the United States of America

What Readers Say

One of the biggest mistakes that I see holding entrepreneurs back is they've got fear around technology or are confused around technology. I always recommend Sue Wilhite because she takes the complexity of technology and simplifies it in a way that people understand. Read her book so you can understand the technology you need in business.

Robert Butwin, Success Strategist
Author, "Street Smart Networking"

This book is amazing! It is simple to read, simple to comprehend, and simple to execute the strategies that Sue Wilhite suggests. Also, she is hilarious, which makes it a fun and most enjoyable read. I am **NOT** a tech person, and assiduously avoid any hint or suggestion of being one, but this book is so easy to follow that even I enjoy it!

Tamir Qadree, Coach, The Dean of Dynamic Results
Author, "Clear Vision: Your Road to Riches"

What a pleasant surprise! Here's a book you can pick and open to any chapter and you're going to learn something valuable and usable. It's organized as a directory of best practices, must-haves, or need-to-knows, and it all comes across in a warm, readable, and personal "Sue style." *Tech Tips for the Tech-Timid* is definitely a reference you'll return to again and again. Nicely done!

Tom Gay, serial tech entrepreneur

As a 40-plus-year techie who learned how to teach tech to her grandpa in the 1990s over the telephone while driving, I wish I would have had *Tech Tips for the Tech-Timid* by Sue Wilhite, to give him for the times I wasn't around! This book is really an easy read, while giving you well-organized information about technology in a world where technology has continued to be fearful to many – young and old alike. It is comprehensive and accessible while also empowering readers to overcome their fears and navigate the digital world with confidence.

Stacy Braiuca, the Change Navigator™
Author, "Unleashing Your Unstoppable Destiny"!

TABLE OF CONTENTS

DEDICATION

To all of those who have believed in me all these years, no matter which path I was on or what direction I went.

To all of YOU who reboot your curiosity and come along for the exploration –

Bravely done!

ACKNOWLEDGMENTS

Gosh, where do I even start?

So many people have helped over the years: all the tech folk who taught and encouraged me; all the mind-body-spirit folk who inspired me (literally, in some cases!); the coaches who kicked my butt into gear and helped me get clear on who I really serve and how.

And of course, my wonderful wife, who's been there for me and believed in me no matter what! I love you!

DISCLAIMER

I had some help with writing this book, which I completely appreciated - yes, it was ChatGPT and other AI that made suggestions about some of the content. In many cases, they were great ideas, and I incorporated them. Others I modified, rewrote, and/or added to.

The process cut short my writing time and saved me from staring at a blinking cursor. You wouldn't be reading this if not for AI. I'd rather have the book in your hands…

WHO'S THIS BOOK FOR?

This book is for small business owners, entrepreneurs, and business owners who are looking to make technology their trusted partner and helper, rather than an unknowable and frustrating enemy.

I especially want to help those who may not be as comfortable or as experienced with technology, but who are eager to learn, willing to be curious, and grow their businesses using the power of tech.

I was blessed with the ability to work with all the parts of my brain: the mystic, woo-woo, so-called "right brain;" and the logical, pattern-seeking, alleged "left-brain[1]." I've been able to translate all the tech jargon into mostly understandable English.

Over the years, I noticed a growing need for easy-to-understand tech advice for people who are uncomfortable or inexperienced with technology. I want to help fill the gap by providing valuable insights and tips for business owners and other tech-timid readers.

Whether you're a freelancer, a consultant, a healing arts practitioner, or a creative professional, this book will provide you with the essential tech hacks you need to streamline your operations and increase your productivity.[1]

---

[1] Neuroscience has dropped most of the division between the halves of the brain, just like the mythical "10%" that we supposedly use. We utilize 100% of our brains, and pretty much all of it can be trained to do pretty much anything! I love brains!

INTRODUCTION

Welcome to *Tech Tips for the Tech-Timid*! You know how challenging it can be to balance all the responsibilities of running a business on your own. With so much to do and so little time, a little knowledge of technology can be a business owner's best friend.

Tech can be frighteningly overwhelming, too. So many tools, so much to learn, so much to keep up with!

I understand the desire to be a Luddite (go look them up: they wanted to banish the wheel for going too far with technology!) and even a Saboteur (go look that up, too - those folks threw their shoes {called "sabots" in French} into the automated looms trying to halt the early Industrial Revolution.

Neither strategy worked, and technology

from forks, knives, and chopsticks to wheels, printing presses, and computers have continued to progress and proliferate. Human beings will always want to extend their reach as long as they have brains to dream up how.

So this book is what I call a "dipping book." You can "dip" into whatever chapter you need or want. You do NOT have to read it cover to cover, although you might flip through the pages to get a sense of what's available.

I'll explore tech hacks and tools in lots of arenas, explaining them as simply as possible, to help you work smarter, not harder, so you can focus on what you do best: growing your business by serving your customers.

But don't worry — I'll do my best to avoid boring you with technical jargon and dry explanations. I approach each topic with a lighthearted, humorous tone, making learning as fun and engaging as possible.

Whether you're a seasoned business owner looking to level up your tech game, or just starting out and feeling overwhelmed, *Tech Tips for the Tech-Timid* has something for you.

By the end of the book, you'll have the skills and knowledge to dramatically increase your productivity, collaborate with others, and protect your online presence.

One more (important) thing: A "tech hack" is a simple and effective way of using technology to make your life easier and more efficient. It's a shortcut, a tip, or a trick that can help you save time and get things done quickly, without having to be a tech expert. Tech hacks can be anything from using keyboard shortcuts or an app to automate a task, to setting up a reminder on your phone, to using a voice assistant like Siri or Alexa to help you stay organized. Hacks simplify your life and help you work smarter, not harder, by leveraging the power of technology. So don't be intimidated by the term "tech hack" - it's simply a way of using technology to your advantage.

Here's one "tech hack" that's really useful to a business owner that you'll see throughout the book: QR Codes. "QR" stands for "Quick Response." You may have seen them on the sides of buses, or if you went out to eat during the pandemic, restaurants used them to display their menu on your phone.

Open up the camera app on your phone and point it to the funky-looking image below.

You don't have to actually take a picture, just center the focus on the image.

You will get a message that it wants to send a text message "TECH" to my phone number. When you say "Yes" to that, you will be pointed to a download page for my "Essential Tech for Business" PDF guide. Nifty, huh?

I'll have some others for you later. They will open websites with more information and resources for you.

Download "Essential Tech for
Business" QR Code

CHAPTER 1

My (Short) Story

When looking back at your life, you will see that the moments which seemed to be great failures followed by wreckage were the incidents that shaped the life you have now.

~ *Joseph Campbell, Mythologist and author of "The Hero with A Thousand Faces"*

Through a series of unexpected twists and turns, my life seems to be (so far!) a journey to integrate technology/science with mind-body-spirit healing and personal development. After decades of study and experience, I have come to the conclusion that it's all the same thing.

But I get it – many business owners find technology more than a little scary and overwhelming. I'd like to share a little bit of my story of how I came to merge the mind-body-spirit world with the realm of technology.

In college, I realized with a heavy heart that my "math block" was causing me to flunk the science classes I needed. In the middle of my sophomore year, I reluctantly changed my major to Comparative Literature. But there were compensations. The books were better written and lighter! Reading a paperback novel by the pool and legitimately calling it "studying" was great!

Spring quarter of my senior year, I ended up taking a class in BASIC programming. It was like finding a hidden treasure chest—I was instantly captivated. I discovered the power of writing simple programs that could effortlessly handle repetitive tasks, leaving me free to focus on other things (like pondering the mysteries of the universe while sipping a cup of tea).

The more I got into programming, the more I enjoyed it. I found it easy - even the "hard" languages like Assembly and RPG. I pursued a two-year degree in management information systems, with a business focus. I went to work for companies all over the Silicon Valley, doing programming, database design, and systems maintenance for nearly every department of every company. I called it "learning business from the inside out."

I was fabulously successful, working my way up to IT Manager, until one day my body rebelled. An ulcer forced me to pause and reevaluate my priorities. After a year of conventional medical treatment, I discovered the wonders of mind-body healing. Without hesitation, I bid farewell to my IT manager position and embarked on a journey of self-discovery, becoming a hypnotherapist and exploring the vast realm of personal growth and healing.

But technology was not left behind! Even as I explored the realms of the mind and spirit, I maintained my connection with the ever-evolving world of bits and bytes. I created online spaces, including early social media and websites, for various organizations I was associated with.

Today, my passions have merged harmoniously, like a celestial dance between mind-body-spirit and technology. As a coach, I offer my expertise and support to those who find themselves bewildered by the intricacies of technology.

With a wave of my digital wand, I help these technologically challenged souls navigate their systems, bringing order to the chaos and ensuring smooth sailing on the vast digital sea.

I find immense joy in helping others with their technology needs. It's like a wonderful dance that connects two different worlds— the magical and the digital. It's a harmonious symphony where our thoughts, our bodies, our spirits, and technology come together.

CHAPTER 2

From Stressed to Zen:
Relaxation and Mindfulness Apps

In this chapter, we'll explore some of the best relaxation and mindfulness apps for busy business owners, and how you can use them to reduce stress and improve your overall well-being.

One of the first things I tell stressed and panicking clients is "Breathe!" Let's ease into technology with apps designed to help you relax. They may become your biggest go-to tech!

As a business owner, it's easy to feel stressed and overwhelmed, but with the help of relaxation and mindfulness apps, you can find peace and clarity any time.

Just taking a few minutes each day to practice, and you will start feeling more relaxed and centered every day. A ton of research (I weighed it!) over the last several decades has demonstrated that a few minutes of mindfulness gives hours of productivity.

Before you think of meditation as a waste of time, let me point out that your brain shuts down all logical and analytical thinking when it's stressed. You actually get less done, and get more distracted without a chance to let your brain reset and recharge. Check out these apps and give yourself space to relax.

Calm

Calm is a popular relaxation and mindfulness app that offers guided meditations, sleep stories, and breathing exercises. With Calm, you can choose from a variety of guided meditations, ranging from 3 to 25 minutes, and even customize your meditation with different background sounds. Calm also offers sleep stories, which are bedtime stories for adults designed to help you fall asleep faster and wake up feeling refreshed. Who doesn't secretly want a bedtime story?

https://www.calm.com/

Headspace

Headspace offers guided meditations and mindfulness exercises. You can choose from a variety of guided meditations ranging from 3 to 30 minutes, and even customize your meditation with different themes, such as stress or focus. Headspace also offers mindfulness exercises, which are short activities designed to help you practice mindfulness throughout the day.

https://www.headspace.com/

Insight Timer

Insight Timer is a meditation app that offers guided meditations as well as a timer for silent meditation. Choose from thousands of guided meditations, from a variety of teachers and traditions. You can also customize your meditation with different background sounds and track your progress over time.

https://insighttimer.com/

The Tapping Solution

The Tapping Solution App is a little gem that can help you manage stress, anxiety, and even physical pain. It's a super easy tool that you can use anywhere, anytime, and it doesn't take much time. You just tap your fingers on certain points on your body while focusing on your specific issue, and before you know it, you'll feel more relaxed and in control. Plus, the app provides guided sessions and helpful resources to help you make the most of your tapping practice.

https://www.thetappingsolution.com/

Aura

Aura is a mindfulness app that offers personalized meditations based on your mood and goals. With Aura, you can choose from a variety of guided meditations, ranging from 3 to 30 minutes, and even customize your meditation with different background sounds. Aura also offers daily reminders and mindfulness exercises designed to help you practice mindfulness throughout the day.

https://www.aurahealth.io/

CHAPTER 3

Time-Saving Tips
to Streamline Your Day

In this chapter, you'll get an overview of some of the ways to get rid of drudgery and the routine tasks that may bog you down.

I personally loathe repetitive work. I could never work on an assembly line, or in food service, or anything that makes me do the same thing all the time. (For those who follow that sort of thing, I'm a 7 on the Enneagram, yes I am!) I fell in love with technology and programming to allow the computer to do things that it did better than I did.

Between running your business and keeping up with your personal life, you're looking to find time for everything on your to-do list. That's where tech hacks really shine! If you've ever wanted to clone yourself, you now have the technology to pretend you have.

Automate Your Tasks

One of the best and most valuable benefits of technology is the ability to automate tasks. Programs like IFTTT ("If This Then That") and Zapier allow you to create automated task sets between different apps and services, so you can focus on more important and personal parts of your business.

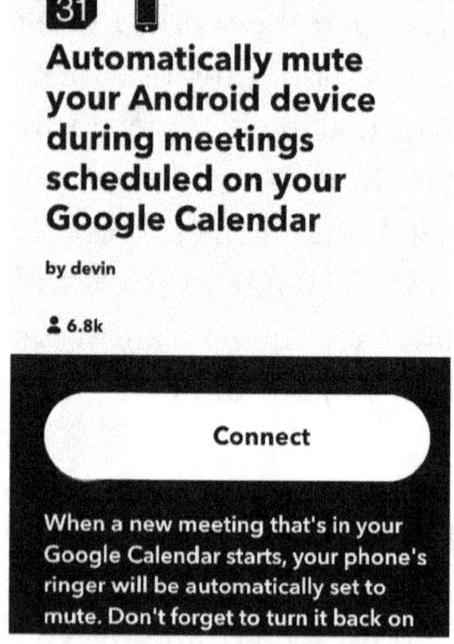

For example, I use IFTTT to automatically mute my phone during every event on my calendar.

For another example, you can create a "workflow" (like a mini-program) that automatically saves email attachments to Google Drive, or that automatically adds new customers to your Customer Relationship Management (you do have a CRM system, right??).

I use Zapier to upload payments from PayPal into a spreadsheet; I could have it go directly to QuickBooks, but I like to monitor transactions before they go "live."

Use Voice Typing
My biggest hangup when creating content is just getting started. I'm great at talking to people, explaining what I do or describing a step-by-step process, but when it comes to sitting down and writing it all out: UGH! Fortunately, technology has come up with the solution. Voice activated assistants like Siri, Alexa, and Google Assistant can be a business owner's best friend. Voice-activated utilities can help you with a variety of tasks, such as setting reminders,

making phone calls, and sending texts - all with the power of your voice. By using voice commands, you can save time and focus on other important tasks, without having to stop what you're doing to complete a simple task.

Whether you type with one or two fingers or you can clatter away with all ten, you probably get caught worrying about spelling and punctuation. Voice assistants will speed up everything! Did you know you can even dictate documents or social media posts with a little bit of practice, saving you a lot of time and lost thoughts.

See this video example on the Resource Guide

Organize Your Inbox

Email is one of the biggest time-wasters for business owners. Between spam emails and irrelevant newsletters, it can be challenging to keep your inbox organized.

Fortunately, there are several tools available that can help you streamline your email inbox. One of these tools is Unroll.me, which allows you to unsubscribe from unwanted emails and combine relevant emails into a single daily digest.

Setting up your daily discipline will give you more energy, since you won't be wasting your attention on all that junk. Go to the Resource Page and check out this brilliant video - it's a little long, but it's SO worth it. I've used her techniques for the last three years, and it's made my email life much better.

Kelly's Amazing Email Organization System

Create Templates

Creating templates for commonly used documents can save you an enormous amount of time. You can find pre-made templates online, many of them for free, so you can complete tasks quickly and efficiently without re-creating the wheel. Setting them up the first time may be an effort, but you will pat yourself on the back every time you use them.

Tools to help you create document templates include Google Docs, Sheets, or

Slides, and JotForm.

Templates also help you keep your branding consistent for your visual assets, like videos and social media posts. Camtasia (a video editor) and Canva (a design tool) also let you create visual templates to reuse over and over.

I use templates for my invoices, presentations, and customer agreements, and for my podcast. I also use templates in Gmail for standard replies or contacts. For example, I have a welcome message for my podcast guests, and another announcing when their show goes live.

Take Advantage of Keyboard Shortcuts

Keyboard shortcuts are a time-saving tool that every business owner should be familiar with - and they only use two or three fingers. By using keyboard shortcuts, you can perform tasks quickly and efficiently, without having to navigate through different menus.

I use **ALT-TAB** all the time: first, it shows you what programs are active at the moment. If you continue to hold the **ALT** key and keep hitting **TAB**, it selects between them.

See the Resource Page for a little video of what it looks like on a Mac…

Some of the most common keyboard shortcuts include:

Action	PC	Mac
Copy	CTRL+C	+C
Paste	CTRL+V	+V
Undo	CTRL+Z	+Z
Paste Special (removes formatting)	CTRL+Shift+V	+Shift+V

What's Paste Special? Have you ever done a copy-and-paste from a website or from one document to another and found weird formatting? That keyboard shortcut removes all formatting, like magic! I use it all the time!

Another little-known shortcut I use has to

do with the "Up" and "Down" and "Left" and "Right" arrows, especially in spreadsheets. Open up a spreadsheet and type some junk into a bunch of cells. Then hold down the **CTRL** key (or the   on the Mac) and hit the arrow key of your choice. You will find you selected the first non-empty cell in that direction.

See the Resource Page for a little video of what it looks like in a Google Sheets document…

In regular documents, it will usually move the cursor a word or a line at a time.

If you hold down the Shift key at the same time (CTRL+Shift+arrow), it will *select* the word or the line. You can keep hitting the arrow key to select more.

More Typing Shortcuts

If you just discovered and fell in love with keyboard shortcuts, my next topic will really make your heart beat faster. Text expanders are like your personal superpower for typing. They allow you to create shortcuts or abbreviations for frequently used words, phrases, or even entire paragraphs. So instead of typing out the same long sentences over and over again, you can just type a simple shortcut, and the text expander magically expands it into the full text you need.

Think of it as having a secret language with your computer. For example, if you often write "Thank you for your interest in our products," you can create a shortcut like "tyip" (short for "thank you interest products"). When you type "tyip" (without quotes) and press a special key, the text expander understands your secret code and instantly turns it into the full sentence. Ta-da! You saved time and energy. Some text expanders, like Typinator (https://ergonis.com/typinator), use the accessibility functions of your computer so you don't even have to have a special key.

They're especially handy when you need to respond quickly to emails or write similar messages to different people.

I like using them to fill out forms. I fill out a lot of speaker applications, and they're always asking for LinkedIn, Facebook, Instagram, websites, bios, etc. I have shortcuts for each of these, so if time is short or a deadline is looming, I can zip through filling out the forms.

So, with text expanders, you can zip through your work like a pro, impressing others with your lightning-fast responses. It's like having a magic wand for your keyboard, making your life much smoother and less tiring.

Use Social Media Management Tools

Facebook, Instagram, LinkedIn, TikTok: social media are fun and useful tools for business owners, but they can also be a significant time and attention suck. Fortunately, there are several social media management tools available that can help you streamline your social media presence. If you have your brand and message dialed in, you can maximize your results.

Using social media management tools like Hootsuite, Buffer, or Sprout Social allow you to schedule posts in advance, monitor mentions and engagement, and track your analytics, all in one place. None of them will guarantee thousands of followers, of course, but you can avoid all the distractions and rabbit holes! They each have free plans, so you can try them out for at least a month and see what works for you.

Invest in a Time-Tracking Tool
Finally, investing in a time-tracking tool can help you gain a better understanding of where your time is going if you're on your computer a lot.

Time-tracking tools allow you to track the time you spend on different tasks, so you can identify areas where you may be wasting time. You can also identify areas to improve your productivity, integrate into other apps, and bill clients accurately for the time you've spent on their projects.

Two popular examples of time-tracking tools are **Toggl** and **RescueTime**.

With **Toggl**, you can start and stop a timer with a single click, assign projects and clients to your time entries, and view detailed reports of your time usage. You can also integrate Toggl with other apps, such as Asana and Trello, to streamline your workflow. Toggl works on multiple platforms, such as Windows, macOS, Android, and iOS.

RescueTime tracks the time you spend on different websites, apps, and tasks, and categorizes them into productive, neutral, or distracting activities. You can set goals for how much time you want to spend on productive activities and receive alerts when you're spending too much time on distracting activities. RescueTime also provides detailed reports on your time usage, including your daily, weekly, and monthly trends. RescueTime works on Windows or macOS computers.

All these time-saving tech hacks can help you streamline your day and maximize your productivity. So go ahead and give these hacks a try – your future self (and perhaps your current family and friends) will thank you!

CHAPTER 4

Streamlining Your Workflow:
Automating Your Business Processes

In this chapter, we'll explore how you can use automation to save time and increase efficiency in your business.

Email Marketing Automation

Email marketing automation can help you save time by automating repetitive tasks, such as sending welcome emails to customers who've signed up to your list, or wishing clients happy birthday at the beginning of the month. There are several email marketing automation tools available, including Mailchimp, ConvertKit, and Aweber. These tools allow you to set up automated email sequences that can help you nurture leads and build relationships with your audience.

Social Media Automation

Social media can be a time-consuming task, but with the help of automation tools, you can save time while still maintaining an active presence on social media. I mention some of the tools in Chapter 3. These tools allow you to schedule posts in advance, monitor your accounts, and engage with your followers, all from a single dashboard.

Appointment Scheduling

If you spend a lot of time scheduling appointments with clients, then an appointment scheduling tool can help you save time. Some popular appointment scheduling tools include Calendly, Acuity, and Book Like a Boss. These tools allow you to set your availability, share your calendar with clients, and even accept payments for appointments. Book Like a Boss is so robust, it can even be used as a basic website!

Invoicing and Payment Automation

Managing your finances can be a time-consuming task, but with the help of invoicing and payment automation tools, you can save time and get paid faster. Some popular invoicing and payment automation tools include FreshBooks, QuickBooks, PayPal, and Stripe. These tools allow you to create and send invoices, accept payments online, and even set up recurring payments.

Project Management Automation

If you're working on multiple projects at once, then a project management tool can help you stay organized and on track. Some popular project management tools include Asana, Trello, and Basecamp. These tools allow you to create and assign tasks, set deadlines, and collaborate with your team, all in one place.

Customer Relationship Management Automation

If you're looking to build stronger relationships with your clients, then a Customer Relationship Management (CRM) tool can help you stay organized and keep track of client interactions. Some CRM tools that I've used include Insightly,

EngagePro, and HubSpot. These tools allow you to store client information, track interactions, and even automate follow-up tasks. Start now, when you've got less to track, and you'll be happier later when sales and prospects pour in!

Full confession: this is my favorite chapter! I had to restrain myself from putting in all the goodies - I didn't want to overwhelm you!

The computer was invented to take the burden off of humans, do repetitive tasks, and keep track of events so we don't have to! Take advantage of automation tools, and free up your time to focus on what you do best – growing your business!

CHAPTER 5

Never Miss a Beat:
Tips for Managing Your Inbox like a Pro

In this chapter, I'll share tips for managing your inbox like a pro, including how to use filters, labels, and canned responses. I'll also cover the importance of email etiquette and how to write effective emails that get results.

Email has been a staple of communication for decades. Even though various instant messaging and collaboration apps like WhatsApp and Slack have come on the scene, email remains a fundamental tool for business communication. I want to be clear that I'm talking about your email inbox, NOT emails sent out as marketing tools.

Books have been written on that topic alone!

Why Use Email Instead of Other Apps?

- **Convenience**: Unlike real-time messaging apps like texting, WhatsApp, or Telegram (let alone an actual phone call!), email allows for "asynchronous communication," meaning that messages can be sent and received at different times. This provides flexibility for both the sender and recipient to respond when it's convenient, accommodating different schedules and time zones.

- **Formality and professionalism**: Email tends to be more formal and professional compared to other communication apps - less emojis, f-bombs, or casual language. It is considered official correspondence for business proposals and client communications. Understanding the more professional nature of email can help you craft appropriate and respectful messages.

- **Record-keeping and/or documentation**: Because they can last forever on server backups, emails serve as an official record of communication, providing a trail of information that can be referenced in the future.

Email Etiquette

Now that you know "why email," I want to talk about what makes a good email. One of my bosses taught me "always make progress." In other words, either wrap up the subject or make sure you're conveying enough information that others can move forward.

- **Use a clear and concise subject line**: A good subject line helps recipients understand the purpose of your email at a glance. Make it specific and informative to enhance the chances of your email being opened and responded to promptly. Good subject line: *"Can we meet on Tuesday morning about X?"* Bad subject line: *"Hey. I need to talk."*
- **Use a professional tone**: Hold off

on the emojis and f-bombs, especially with people you don't know well. Use proper greetings, salutations, and respectful language. Avoid slang, abbreviations, jargon, or overly casual language that might be perceived as unprofessional.

- **Keep your emails brief and focused**: Respect your recipients' time by keeping your emails concise and to the point. Use paragraphs and bullet points to break up information and make it easier to read and understand.

- **Be mindful of grammar and spelling**: Most email programs now have grammar and/or spelling checks built in. Even if you have spell-check, take the time to proofread your emails before clicking Send, or ask a colleague to review particularly sensitive/important emails.

- **Pro Tip**: Gmail has an UNDO feature for emails that you can configure. Click the Settings button (looks like a gear), then look for "Undo Send" - it was about the 4th item down the last time I checked. I set mine to 30 seconds; your time may vary. Be sure to Save the settings. Then next time you click "Send," look for the little banner at the bottom of the page that says "Undo Send?" It lasts for as long as you configured it for **-OR-** the next time you open an email/folder

- **Don't "Reply All" unless you really mean to.** We've all heard horror stories about unintended recipients! You can configure most email programs to default to just Reply. *Please*, make sure you've done that.

- **Respond promptly and courteously**: Do your best to respond to emails in a timely manner, even if it's just to acknowledge receipt and indicate when you'll provide a detailed response. Remember the Undo feature if you get carried away.

- **Use professional email signatures**: Include your name, job title, contact information, and any relevant links or social media profiles. There's lots of good templates out there for signatures.

Setting Up an Effective Email System

You can achieve Inbox Zero with just a few clicks, and maintain it forever with just a little discipline. Don't lose important information because you don't know where you put it - let your email program do all the work!

Another important aspect of email management: remember that you control the inbox, the inbox does NOT control you. Unless you're in a support role, resist checking your inbox every five minutes. Make a rule that works for you: once a day, twice a day, maybe three times a day. Trust me, it lowers your blood pressure to not be scanning all the time!

Establish a clear folder structure: Learn how to create folders and organize your emails into categories that make sense for your business. I create folders for Finance [all my receipts and invoices and payment notices go in here], for long term projects, for topics like AI, Tech Support, and groups I belong to. Gmail allows me not only to have folders, but to tag emails with multiple categories. I can have something labeled "Finance" and tagged as "Website" for my annual hosting and domain emails.

Utilize filters and rules: Biggest time saver ever! It may take most of an afternoon to set up, but you'll save MONTHS of time. You can set up filters and rules to automatically sort incoming emails into specific folders based on criteria like who sent it, subject line (whole or part), or keywords within the email body. For example, I have filters in Gmail that notice my automatic monthly payments to different vendors and just stick them in the "Finance" folder automatically. I don't need to see them!

Master the art of email triage: Develop a systematic approach for quickly scanning and prioritizing incoming emails. Flag urgent messages with stars or other tools of your email program, unsubscribe from irrelevant newsletters as fast as possible, and use email preview features whenever possible.

Explore and play with email

management tools: Different email programs have different management tools available. You might have features such as snooze options (you'll get to that email tomorrow, you promise - click Snooze for a particular time for it to nudge you), email scheduling (send that email after office hours for you, but well within your recipient's), and email tracking (did they actually open that email, and when?). Become curious and look for them!

Create templates and canned responses: I had two templates for my podcast guests: one welcoming them and another telling them when the show was live. I have templates for initiating cold speaking opportunity inquiries. If you find yourself answering the same question frequently, that sounds like a template to me! You can always edit and customize the templates once in the editor, so they don't sound completely canned and impersonal.

CHAPTER 6

Stay Connected:
Be Productive on the Go

In this chapter, we'll explore the top apps that even the most tech-timid person needs to have on their phone or tablet. Note: In this chapter, whenever I mention "phone," I mean "phone or tablet."

As a business owner, you're constantly on the go. Whether you're meeting with clients, attending networking events, or working from a coffee shop, you need access to essential apps that can help you stay connected and productive.

Communication Apps
Do you need to stay connected to clients, vendors, or colleagues without losing everything in an overcrowded email inbox?

Communication apps allow you to stay connected with clients and colleagues. These apps allow you to send messages, make phone calls, and even conduct video conferences, all from your phone.

Two of the most popular communication apps (and ones that I really like) are **WhatsApp** and **Slack**.

WhatsApp seems to be just like texting, but has more powerful features and benefits. WhatsApp can send secure (i.e., less hackable/trackable) messages, pictures, and even videos. In addition, WhatsApp uses the internet (WiFi) to send messages, while standard texting uses the cellular network. With WhatsApp, you can send messages to people all around the world without having to pay extra fees for international texting. WhatsApp allows you to create groups where you can chat with multiple people at once. For example, you can set up group projects, coordinate events with multiple people more easily, or create a way for your course attendees to interact with each other.

Slack does even more: think of Slack as a

virtual office where you can not only send messages and make video calls with your colleagues, you can also share files. A lot of big companies use Slack to manage remote work, and that means it's really easy to use (because who has time for training?).

Email Apps

Email is a critical part of any business owner's workflow. It's how you communicate with clients, send proposals, and manage your schedule. To stay on top of your email inbox, it's essential to have a reliable email app on your phone. Some popular email apps include Gmail, Outlook, and Apple Mail. These apps allow you to manage your inbox, send and receive emails, and even schedule emails to be sent at a later time.

It's important to differentiate between email apps like those listed above, and marketing apps like Constant Contact or Mailchimp. *Marketing apps* help you get your brand message across to your customer and prospects via newsletters. *Email* is for one-to-few communications, and usually very specific subjects.

Productivity Apps

Productivity apps can help you stay organized and on top of your to-do list. There are several types of productivity apps available, including note-taking apps, task management apps, and project management apps. Some popular productivity apps include Evernote, Todoist, and Asana (links are on the Resource page). These apps allow you to create and manage tasks, set reminders, and collaborate with others, all from your phone. They all do pretty much the same thing in the same way, just the interface differs.

Some productivity apps base themselves around popular productivity systems, like Getting Things Done (GTD) by David Allen or the Pomodoro Method by Francesco Cirillo. Don't worry if you don't know all the terminology from either of these - the apps will help you out!

Social Media Apps

Social media is a powerful tool for business owners, but it can also be a significant time drain. To stay on top of your social media presence, it's essential to have social media apps on your phone. Some popular social media apps include Facebook, Twitter, and LinkedIn. These apps allow you to manage your accounts, schedule posts, and engage with your followers, all from your phone.

Design Apps

Visual content is becoming increasingly important in today's digital age. Whether you're creating social media graphics or designing your website, having a design app on your phone can be incredibly helpful. Some popular design apps include Canva, Adobe Spark, and PicMonkey. These apps allow you to create stunning graphics and designs, all from your phone.

Travel Apps

As a business owner, you may find yourself traveling frequently for business. Make your travels more manageable, by loading a few travel apps on your phone. Travel apps like Expedia, Airbnb, and TripIt allow you to book flights and accommodations, manage your itinerary, and even track your expenses, all from your phone. Rideshare apps like Lyft and Uber can help you get short trips handled, and even Doordash and Instacart can come in handy in an out-of-the-way hotel with no room service!

CHAPTER 7

Protecting Yourself Online:
Cybersecurity Tips for everyone

In this chapter, we'll explore cybersecurity tips that every business owner should be aware of. And, oh yeah - they work for your personal life, too!

In the 21st century, your online presence is critical to the success of your business. It's how you can reach new clients, communicate with your audience, and manage your finances. However, with the rise of cyber threats, it's essential to protect your online presence from potential attacks.

Use Strong Passwords
Your birthday is not a good password! Your dog's name, your children's initials make horrible passwords. I can't stress this enough! I was really obnoxious in my

corporate jobs about making sure people didn't leave sticky notes with their passwords on their monitors! The first and most critical step in protecting your online presence is to use strong passwords. Your password is your first line of defense against cyber threats, and a weak password can make it easy for hackers to gain access to your accounts.

To create a strong password, use a combination of letters, numbers, and symbols, and avoid using personal information. You should (must) also use different passwords for different accounts, so if one account is compromised, your other accounts will still be secure.

I use a fun hack for creating passwords: think of phrases, uncommon or less popular book titles, or short sentences that you can remember easily. Use the first letters of the words, substituting numbers and special characters as appropriate.

For example, Dale Carnegie's book "How to Win Friends and Influence People" could be made into dch7Wf&1p (which includes his initials at the beginning. You could do it backwards, or put his initials at the end, or change up the capital and lowercase letters.

However, I ***strongly*** recommend a password management system, like LastPass, Dashlane, or Keeper. They will generate and remember longer random passwords for you. The recommended length of passwords as of May 2023 is about 14 characters.

Enable Two-Factor Authentication (2FA)

Two-factor authentication is an additional layer of security that requires you to provide two forms of identification to access your accounts. This can be something you know (like a password) plus something you have (like a code sent to your phone).

Two-factor authentication adds an extra layer of protection to your accounts and can prevent hackers from gaining access, even if they have your password.

Google has a two-factor authenticator for Android phones that you can use for many online apps. More and more online apps have been implementing and insisting on 2FA, so you might want to adopt it sooner than later. The app generates a multi-digit code every 30 seconds or minute that you use right away to login.

Keep Everything Up to Date

Software updates often include security patches that fix known vulnerabilities, so that your devices are protected against the latest cyber threats. **Make sure to update your operating system, applications, antivirus software, and any website plugins regularly. (See Chapter 11.)**

Use Antivirus Software

And speaking of that, antivirus software can help protect your computer against malware, viruses, and other cyber threats. Make sure to use reputable antivirus software and keep it up to date. You should also run regular (daily, or even twice daily if you're really paranoid) scans to check for any potential threats.

Don't Click That Link! REALLY!

Cybercriminals send "phishing" emails or

texts to gain access to your accounts. They look authentic, using copied logos and legit-sounding writing. One method includes a link that leads to a fake website designed to steal your personal information. Another is to include a document that looks like an invoice or other official notice to get you to download it.

Always double-check the sender's email address and/or URL to make sure it's legitimate before entering any personal information. Use your mouse to just hover over the email address - **DON'T** click it - and you will see if it has nothing to do with the purported sender.

As of this writing, Google has just started an email authentication program for companies to verify real emails in Gmail. For my part, I try to send along suspicious emails or links to the real company's legal team.

Back up Your Data
Have you backed up your hard drive today? How about your website? How about your phone? Most importantly, do you know

how to restore them? (*What, again? Didn't I say that already? Yep.*)

In the event of a cyber attack or a hardware failure, having a backup of your important data can prevent you from losing everything. Make sure to back up your data regularly and store it in at least two different secure locations: online and offline. You can back up your data to an external hard drive and cloud storage service like Google Drive. I recommend **iDrive** as one of the least expensive, most robust, and easy to use on any platform: https://www.idrive.com

Educate Yourself on Cybersecurity
Finally, it's essential to learn cybersecurity best practices, at least the basics. By understanding the different types of cyber threats and how to protect yourself against them, you can ensure that your online presence remains secure. Use your favorite search engine to seek out online courses and webinars that can help you stay up to date on the latest cybersecurity trends.

Whew! Feeling anxious yet? Take a deep breath, then take the necessary steps to protect your online presence – your business and your clients will thank you for it! (And perhaps check Chapter 2 for some calming apps.)

CHAPTER 8

Mastering Google:
Use Google's Free Tools to Streamline Your Business

In this chapter, we'll explore Google tools for business, and how you can use them to streamline your workflow and grow your business.

Google is more than just a search engine – it offers a suite of free tools that can help you streamline your business and save time.

Google Drive
Google Drive is a cloud storage platform that allows you to create, edit, store, and share all kinds of files via the internet. You can access your files from anywhere (even your phone or tablet) and collaborate with others in real-time (it's completely mind-

blowing to observe multiple people typing in the same document).

Some of the best features of Google Drive include:

- 15 GB of free storage (as of this writing); you can upgrade to near-infinite storage for a small monthly fee.

- Includes Google tools, such as Docs and Sheets, as well as others available through the Marketplace

- Real-time collaboration with others

- Easy sharing with customizable access levels

Google Calendar
I love Google Calendar! More than just a datebook, it can keep you more organized than you thought possible. With Google Calendar, you can (of course) create events, set reminders, and invite others to events.

My favorite feature of Google Calendar: you can create multiple "calendars" in the same calendar.

For example, I have my regular appointments that integrate with various other utilities (more about that later). And I also have an "Event Planning Calendar" that I use to plan out when things need to happen in the course of launching an event. I have a "Finance Calendar" to remind me of some monthly and annual payments for things like website and domain renewals or my annual Adobe subscription, so I don't forget and mess up my budget. I have assigned different colors to those calendars so they show up clearly.

Google shows local holidays (for example, US or UK), and you can also integrate other calendars like phases of the moon, sports events, or other interests.

Other great features of Google Calendar include:

- Integration with Gmail

- Easy integration with most appointment creation tools, like Acuity, Book Like a Boss, or Calendly

- Customizable event reminders: how

long before an event, and whether to get them by text or email.

- Ability to share your calendar with others (and vice versa - your family can share with you to keep everyone on the same page!)

- Automatic syncing among your devices (computer, phone, and tablet)

Google Business Profile (formerly Google My Business)

One of the most underutilized free Google tools, Google Business Profile helps you take the online stage and make your presence known. You will be so amazed, you may find yourself saying, "Wow, I can do that?"

You've probably used it multiple times and not even realized it. Let's say you're strolling through a bustling neighborhood, and you suddenly crave a delicious slice of pizza. What do you do? You whip out your trusty smartphone, tap a few keys, and ta-da! Google Business Profile appears, ready to serve you a piping hot slice of convenience. You probably take it totally for granted, and you never thought that your business can have the same magic.

Benefits of Google Business Profile:

- **Attract New Customers**: By showcasing your enticing photos, glowing reviews, and up-to-date business information, you'll have curious customers knocking on your digital door in no time.

- **Build Customer Trust**: The power of positive reviews cannot be underestimated. Google Business Profile allows your happy customers to shower you with five-star love, building trust and credibility for your business.

- **Your Business Profile**: Create a vibrant and eye-catching business profile that reflects your personality. Add your business name, address, phone number, and professional photos that'll make customers want to work with you immediately.

- **Reviews that Rock**: Monitor and respond to customer reviews like a rockstar: show your appreciation to happy customers and address any concerns with grace and charm.

- **Dazzling Insights**: Gain valuable information about how customers find and interact with your business: who looked and went away? Who clicked on your website? Uncover the secret code of customer behavior and make data-driven decisions like a boss.

- **Posting Power**: Google Business Profile (GBP) is like having your very own digital billboard where you can share the latest news, promotions, and events with the world. GBP lets you post updates that'll make customers go, "Ooh, I've got to check that out!"

- **Handy Messaging**: If communicating directly with your prospects and/or customers works for your business, you can enable messaging. Answer questions, provide directions, and sprinkle a dash of customer service magic. It's like having a pocket-sized customer service wizard!

CHAPTER 9

Ditch Your Website
Save Time and Money with Digital Alternatives

In this chapter, we'll explore some of the best digital alternatives to traditional websites, and how you can use them to streamline your online presence and grow your business.

You might have been told — and have seen a lot of evidence for — that having a website is necessary to have an online presence. However, creating and maintaining a website can be time-consuming and costly. Luckily, there are digital alternatives that can help you save time and money, while still reaching your target audience. One caveat: you want to make sure you have **backups** for any content that you have on these sites - take screenshots whenever something significant happens.

Social Media

Social media platforms like Facebook, Instagram, and Twitter can be a great alternative to a traditional website. With social media, you can create a profile that showcases your business, share updates and promotions, and even sell products directly on the platform.

Some benefits of using social media include:

- Lower cost – social media profiles are free to create and maintain

- Built-in audience – social media platforms have millions of users, giving you access to a large potential customer base when used properly

- Easy to update – social media profiles are easy to update with new content and promotions

Landing Pages

Landing pages are single web pages that

are designed to capture a visitor's attention and encourage them to take a specific action, such as signing up for a newsletter or purchasing a product. Landing pages are typically much simpler than full websites, and can be created quickly and easily using tools like Leadpages or Unbounce. Some features of using landing pages include:

- Lower cost – landing pages are often cheaper to create and maintain than full websites

- Faster creation time – landing pages can be created quickly and easily using templates and drag-and-drop editors

- Higher conversion rates – landing pages are designed to be focused and persuasive, which can lead to higher conversion rates for specific actions

Business Listings

Business listings are directories that showcase your business information, such as your address, phone number, and hours of operation. These directories can be a great way to increase your online visibility and reach potential customers who are searching for businesses like yours.

Some popular business listings include:

- Google Business Profile (formerly *Google My Business*) – a free business listing that appears on Google Maps and in Google search results (explored in more detail in Chapter 7)

- Yelp – a popular review site that allows businesses to create a profile and respond to customer reviews

- Yellow Pages – an online directory that lists businesses by category and location. Yes, it still exists!

Digital Business Cards

Have you ever gone to an in-person networking event, collected a bunch of business cards, and handed out your own? And then, a couple of months later, you're looking for that guy who does carpet cleaning - where did you put his card? When did you meet him, and at what event? Although scanning programs help enter information, most people seldom use them. (Full disclosure: I have a plastic box filled with minimally organized paper business cards.)

I was thrilled when I got my first digital business card from HiHello (See Resource Page) just before the COVID pandemic shut down all in-person networking. I had a HUGE advantage since I didn't have to type all my info "in the chat" during virtual networking, just the link to my card.

Digital business cards are essentially online versions of traditional paper business cards. They typically include your name, contact information, and a brief description of your business. Many also include content or links to content like your YouTube or Vimeo channel, chapters from your book, or a mini-blog.

Other digital business card platforms include Linq or LinkTree, and can be shared via email or social media. (See Resource Page for links to these and others.)

Why use digital business cards?

- Eco-friendly – Fewer trees are destroyed than with traditional paper business cards

- Easy to share – digital business cards can be shared quickly and easily via email or social media, or via QR codes in person (See the Introduction for what QR codes are.)

- Convenient – digital business cards can be accessed on any device with an internet connection, making it easy for potential customers to save your information for future reference

- You can put them in your social media bio, online bio, or email signature

CHAPTER 10

Video Conference like a Boss:
How to Ace Virtual Meetings

In this chapter, we'll explore how you can ace virtual meetings and communicate like a pro, using common video conferencing tools.

With the rise of remote work, video conferencing has become an essential tool for communicating with colleagues, clients, and customers. However, virtual meetings can be intimidating, especially if you're not familiar with the technology or best practices.

Setting Up Your Environment

Have you ever been in a meeting where one of the attendees is slightly off camera, or in a cluttered room, or sounds like they're underwater? Any one of those factors makes everyone in the meeting uncomfortable, as well as distracting from their information. In order to be a virtual meeting ace, you must have a professional environment.

Prepare Your Equipment

In addition to having a professional environment, it's important to make sure your equipment is working properly. Before any meeting, test your equipment, including your camera, microphone, and speakers. Make sure you have a stable internet connection and that you're using the latest version of the video conferencing software.

For a complete course in how to set up your space for the best effect, I highly recommend Gary Rogers' webcam workshop. He's a pro, very knowledgeable, and a great teacher. https://suewilhite--companyflix.thrivecart.com/free-webcam-workshop/

Lighting

Good lighting is crucial for successful video conferencing. It can enhance the quality of the video (especially if you're using a digital background) and make it easier for others to see you.

- Make sure your face is well-lit, and avoid backlighting by…
  - Making sure to position the light source in front of you to avoid harsh shadows and ensure a clear and flattering video image, and….

  - Steering clear of windows or other strong lighting behind you, since you'll get washed out like an anonymous witness.

Here are some more suggestions for good lighting:

Natural Light
Natural light is the best lighting option for video conferencing, as it provides a soft and flattering light that is easy on the eyes. Sit facing a window or natural light source.

Ring Light
A ring light is a circular light that can be attached to your webcam or set up separately. It provides even lighting and

eliminates harsh shadows. Here's an example of a ring light: https://www.amazon.com/dp/B08LB8WPRM/

A selfie ring light is a smaller light that can be attached to your phone or laptop, making it a great option for video conferencing on-the-go. Here's an example of a selfie ring light: https://www.amazon.com/dp/B07WYG7V12/

Desk Lamp

A desk lamp can also be a good lighting option for video conferencing, as it can be positioned to provide direct light on your face. Choose a lamp with a bright LED bulb and a flexible arm, such as this one: https://www.amazon.com/dp/B07M6Q1QZB/

Softbox Lighting

Softbox lighting is a professional-grade lighting option that can provide even and diffused light. It consists of a box-shaped light fixture and a diffuser that softens the light. Here's an example of a softbox lighting kit:

https://www.amazon.com/dp/B08MWFV5BK/

Background

Choose a neutral, uncluttered background that won't distract from you or your message. Avoid blinking lights or kinetic sculptures, and anything that looks like it's growing from your body or stabbing you.

If worse comes to worst, Zoom allows you to blur your background, keeping you in focus as long as you're centered, well-lit, and close to the camera. If you move, you may get cut off.

Greenscreen

If you're using a digital background, consider investing in a "greenscreen" or "bluescreen," a mono-colored backdrop typically used in video production that allows video magic to replace the background with whatever picture you like (or you can even use video, although I don't recommend that - it's too distracting).

Make sure you know your space measurements so you get something that will fit your environment.

Here's an example of the greenscreen type I got; there are several formats to choose from:
https://www.amazon.com/dp/B086LC18Q4/ref=sspa_dk_detail_6

Drape

You can use something other than green or blue, and avoid the digital "fuzz" that happens when you try to show-and-tell. A photo drape background can look very professional. Here's an example:

https://www.amazon.com/Maijoeyy-Bookshelf-Background-Conference-Decoration/dp/B08L4VZM8T/ref=sr_1_3

Sound

People will put up with funky video quality but not bad, scratchy, or stuttery sound. Use a high-quality microphone or headset to ensure clear audio.

Start with a stand mic, or one that clips to your laptop. A lavalier or lapel mic is great, but is visible without a lot of wardrobe adjustment; it also ties you to your computer. A good quality microphone can greatly enhance the audio quality of your video calls, even if you're using your laptop or phone as your webcam.

Some good microphones, ranging from pricey to inexpensive, with a variety of connection options, depending on how you plan to be online:

- Jabra Speak 710 - If price is no object, you can get a higher-end, portable, Bluetooth speakerphone with a built-in microphone that delivers clear audio for video conferencing. It can connect to your laptop, phone, or tablet wirelessly and will run you around $300. https://www.jabra.com/business/spe akerphones/jabra-speak-series/jabra-speak-710

- Blue Snowball iCE - This is a popular, simple plug-and-play USB microphone that delivers high-quality audio for video conferencing, podcasting, and more. Weirdly, even though it's called "Blue Snowball," it only comes in black or white! I had one for years before I changed to a lavalier/lapel mic. The Blue Snowball will run you around $50. https://www.bluedesigns.com/produ cts/snowball-ice/

- RoyAroma Lavalier/Lapel Mic - An omnidirectional pick up microphone with intelligent noise reduction that effectively filters noise in the background. This is my current mic, because the sound is so good, and it only costs around $25. https://www.amazon.com/gp/produc t/B08SJZJZRM/ref=ppx_yo_dt_b_a sin_title_o03_s00

- Samson Go Mic - This is a portable USB microphone that can clip onto your laptop or sit on your desk. It delivers high-quality audio for video conferencing, podcasting, and more. It is priced around $50. https://www.samsontech.com/samso n/products/microphones/usb-microphones/gomic/

- Shure MV88 - This is a portable, iOS-compatible microphone that can be used with your iPhone or iPad for high-quality audio recording and video conferencing. It has adjustable stereo width and polar patterns and is priced around $150. https://www.shure.com/en-US/products/microphones/motiv/mv88

- Rode VideoMic Me-L - A good inexpensive directional microphone that connects to your iPhone or iPad for high-quality audio recording and video conferencing. It has a compact design and generally goes for $80. https://www.rode.com/microphones/videomicmel

Practice Good Etiquette

When it comes to virtual meetings, there are certain best practices that you should follow to ensure a smooth and productive meeting. My tips for virtual meeting etiquette:

- Mute your microphone when you're not speaking to avoid background noise.

- Don't be that person who takes their phone into the bathroom with you!

- Use the chat feature to ask questions or make comments, unless the host or moderator says otherwise. But don't "spam the chat" with your stuff

- Avoid multitasking during the meeting, and give your full attention to the discussion. The audience and/or host can tell when you're not looking at the camera because you're making those funny faces and talking to yourself.

- Dress appropriately for the meeting. *Important Note*: If you're using a green- or blue-screen backdrop, avoid wearing that color, or you'll disappear!

Engage Your Audience

Would you invite people to your house, and then monologue at them? Of course not! Wouldn't you show them around, let them know where the beverages and bathrooms are? Of course you would!

If you're the host of a Zoom meeting, it's just as important to be aware of your audience's needs and keep them interested and engaged in the discussion. Some ways to engage your audience:

- Keep sessions under 90 minutes, or schedule breaks every hour and a half. Brains stop processing after about an hour. By the 90-minute mark, fatigue prevents retention or new ideas from forming

- Don't monologue. Instead, allow your audience to chime in. One effective technique I've seen was to allow participants to choose the next topic or direction of the discussion from a short list (no more than three choices)

- Use visual aids like slides or a whiteboard to illustrate your points. But don't just read the slides - BORING! They should be for enhancing what you say, not acting as a teleprompter

- Ask open-ended questions to

encourage discussion and participation

- Use humor or personal anecdotes to make the discussion more engaging

- Summarize key points or action items at the end of the meeting, making sure attendees understand

I strongly recommend Robbie Samuel's book *Break Out of Boredom: Low-Tech Solutions for Highly Engaging Zoom Events* - he's a world-wide expert on virtual meetings, runs a monthly "No More Bad Zoom" meeting, and his book is a real gem. www.BreakOutofBoredom.com

Follow Up
After the virtual meeting, it's vitally important to follow up with any action items or next steps. You don't want people to forget you. Or worse, make them think you forgot them!

Send a thank you email or use a customer management tool like EngagePro, Insightly, or Hubspot to further engage them. Following up after the meeting shows your colleagues or clients that you take their time and input seriously. You move the conversation forward, make progress, and ensure that the session leads to tangible results.

Did you "save the chat?" (See this video to learn how - skip to about 1:25 to miss all the Zoom host meeting setup options: https://youtu.be/yFtetCAlFOk?t=79)

If you have a bunch of chats languishing on your hard drive, and feel overwhelmed with trying to search through them, Chatbridge is here to help! With a few clicks, you can have the chat organized by attendee name and what they posted! You can then upload that to your CRM (it integrates with EngagePro).
https://chatbridgeconnect.com/?aff=positively

CHAPTER 11

Keep Your Tech Up to Date:
Tips for Maintaining Your Devices

In this chapter, we'll explore tips and tools for maintaining your digital life, including your computer, phone, and other gadgets and apps.

Keeping your tech up to date is crucial for maintaining the performance and security of your devices. However, with the constant stream of updates and new devices, it can be difficult to keep up.

Update Your Software

One of the most important things you can do to maintain your devices is to keep your software up to date. This includes your operating system, applications, and antivirus software. By updating your software regularly, you'll ensure that your devices are running smoothly and that any security vulnerabilities are addressed. Most programs will prompt you to update automatically, but you can also manually check for updates, either by clicking on the About… menu item or the Help… menu. Keep a record of what you've upgraded: date, from what version to what version, etc. Spreadsheets work great for keeping track of these.

Keep Your Hardware Clean

Another important aspect of maintaining your devices is keeping them clean. This includes cleaning your screen, keyboard, and other hardware components. You can use a microfiber cloth or a screen-cleaning solution to remove dirt and smudges from your screen, and a can of compressed air to squirt out dust and debris from your keyboard and other hardware components.

Uninstall Unused Programs

Over time, you may accumulate a lot of unused programs on your computer or phone. They take up valuable storage space and slow down your device's performance. It's a good idea to regularly uninstall any programs or apps that you no longer use. On a Windows computer, you go to Settings, then choose Apps, then choose "Uninstall." On a Mac, you can scroll through the "Applications" folder and "Move to Trash" any unused or old programs.

Backup Your Data

(Yes, I said this already. *I can't say it enough*. I've had too many frantic phone calls from clients with failed/hacked systems.) Backing up your data is an essential part of maintaining your devices, as it ensures that your important files and documents are protected in case of a hardware failure or other issue. Also, test your restoration process - you don't want to find out that you can't restore your precious backup!

Use Diagnostic Tools

Most devices come with built-in diagnostic tools that can help you identify and resolve any issues. For example, Windows has a built-in "Task Manager" that shows you which programs and processes are running on your computer, and Mac has a built-in "Activity Monitor" that provides similar information. You can also use third-party diagnostic tools like CCleaner or Malwarebytes to scan your computer for malware and other issues.

Upgrade Your Hardware

If your device is outdated or no longer meets your needs, upgrading your hardware can be a good solution. This may include upgrading your memory (RAM), hard drive, or graphics card on a computer, or replacing your battery on a phone. Always get the most RAM you can afford - even a little bit more that you can afford! Word of warning: before upgrading, make sure to research compatibility and consider consulting with a professional.

CHAPTER 12

How to Troubleshoot Common Tech Issues

In this chapter, you will learn an easy process to troubleshoot pesky problems, as well as online resources, user forums, or professional services that can help you resolve your tech headaches quickly and efficiently.

Scenario 1: When I upgraded the operating system for my Mac laptop recently, and suddenly a bunch of programs stopped working. I had to upgrade them or find alternatives. I've had more than my usual share of program crashes, and knowing that I just upgraded made it easier to troubleshoot.

Scenario 2: A client's website stopped working because new versions of the plugins became available, and they didn't know that they needed to upgrade, or even what to do about it. His web designer had "set up and forgot" about the whole thing.

When tech problems arise, you want to get up and running as quickly as possible. Learning how to troubleshoot common issues can bring you peace of mind and confidence, as well as making you able to communicate effectively with any other tech support.

My number one tip for troubleshooting (besides taking a deep breath; see the calming apps in Chapter 2) is to be curious rather than be frustrated. I *know* these things always break when you've got a deadline, or at the most embarrassing moments, but anger and frustration shut down your brain and keep you from thinking properly.

Saying to yourself "Huh, I wonder what's happening here?" and being curious allows you to notice things that you would miss when you're freaked out and upset.

Keeping a sense of humor helps, too. When I was working in a corporate job, I used to make it my goal to make the tech support person laugh - no matter how serious the issue or how many people were screaming at me to "FIX IT!" Over the years, I got much better support and even some really, really fast escalation in an emergency because tech support *liked* me!

Speaking of a sense of humor: a long-running joke in the tech support community has to do with the first two questions to ask:

Is it plugged in?
Is it turned on?

What to Say to Tech Support

Typically, when someone contacts tech support, they just say: "X isn't working!" Given the wide range of what "not working" can mean, you can understand why the two questions became popular!

Try narrowing down the "not working" part by noticing the following:

- What did you *just* do before it stopped working as expected? What keystroke, tap, or button was done? I know, that means being aware of what you were doing, but give it your best guess.

- What *exactly* is happening now? Is the screen blank, black, or blue? Are things blinking, making noise, or smoking? Is there a message on the screen? If there is, take a picture of it somehow!

- What did you *expect* to happen when you did that? Should an app launch, should a screen close, should a sound play/stop playing, should a menu appear, etc?

- What else is happening on the hardware or software? What other apps or programs were running, or did it shut down completely?

- And, most importantly, what hardware and/or operating system and their versions are you using? **Pro Tip**: *Write these down somewhere easily accessible, separate from the machine they refer to. In other words, save a list of your computer's hardware and* *software on your phone or tablet or easily accessible paper. Take a screenshot after every upgrade. Do the same for your phone/tablet, but save those on your computer.* See the Resource Page *for a little little "helper" I created for the purpose.*

Wi-Fi Connectivity Problems
I admit it - I failed the Networking class when I was getting my degree in Management Information Systems. My transcript says I got an A, but that was because the instructor screwed up, and made up for it by having anyone who turned in a final test get an A for the class. I've gotten better by practical, in-the-field experience, but still - not my favorite tech by any means!

Wi-Fi connectivity issues are hands down one of the most frustrating tech issues to deal with, especially when you're trying to work on important projects or connect with clients, and suddenly you can't connect to email, or your online document, or social media.

Some common causes of Wi-Fi connectivity problems include signal interference, outdated drivers, or router issues. But wait - what does any of that mean, in English! Hang on - I've got you!

Let me make it simple…here, have a picture!

Here is your one-minute Networking lesson for today (with apologies to Mug Old Fashioned Root Beer!):

Stuff is zipping around the Internet. We can tap into that "stuff" by connecting a Modem to it. The Modem comes from your Internet Service Provider (ISP). It "channels" the internet to your location. A Router uniquely identifies your location by giving it a special number called an IP Address (usually a string of numbers that look something like 1.20.300.40.5 - not a real IP Address, I think!).

A Router sends the Internet to your device, either by direct wiring (usually called Ethernet) or over the airwaves - called WiFi. Sometimes, an ISP will give you a device that has the Modem and the Router together; they usually tell you or have it in their paperwork. I don't like those, but many tech people do.

There - now you know everything you need to know about networking!

Assuming your system is working properly right now, walk over to your Modem and Router, and look carefully: see what lights are blinking and what's plugged in where. Get a picture of what's normal and OK so when something goes wrong, you can tell the difference!

Here are some tips for troubleshooting your Wi-Fi signal and improving overall connectivity. They range from simple to somewhat more complicated, and some steps take a chunk of time to complete. **Remember to breathe!**

Check DownDetector.com: A worldwide online program that's a true blessing - I now check that first, looking up my ISP to see if there are any problems reported. Any internet program or service (like Quickbooks or Facebook) can be tracked, not just your ISP. *If there are no problems reported…*

Check Your Wi-Fi Network Settings: The first step in troubleshooting Wi-Fi issues is to check your Wi-Fi network settings on your computer. Look for and click on the Wi-Fi icon: which may be upright like this one, or sideways.

Make sure that your device is connected to the correct network, and that the network is in range and has a strong signal. *If that doesn't work…*

Disable (Turn off) and Re-Enable (Turn on) Wi-Fi on Your Device: This can sometimes help reset your device's network settings and resolve connectivity issues. *If that doesn't work…*

Restart Your Device: Always a favorite answer in tech support: reboot! Sometimes simply restarting your device can help resolve pesky Wi-Fi issues (as well as some others!). Try turning your device off completely, and then back on again to see if that resolves the issue. *If that doesn't work…*

Restart Your Router: First, check that it's plugged in and turned on! (I've been embarrassed by having my Router plugged into a battery backup that ran out of juice.) If your Router is separate from your Modem, do this first! Find the Power button and press it. Lights on the panel should go out. Wait a couple of minutes, then press the Power button again to turn it back on. It always takes several minutes for the Router to fully engage, so be patient. *If that doesn't work…*

Restart Your Modem: **If you need to do this step, turn OFF your Router first**. The Modem may have a Power button, but it may also just have to be unplugged. Again, wait for a few minutes before pressing the Power button or plugging it back in. And wait for at least five (5) minutes for the Modem to fully start up again. When the Modem finishes restarting, turn your Router back on.

If none of those work, there's something more complicated going on. I'm so sorry, you're not going to get that project done in the next 20 minutes…

Check for Software Updates: Outdated software can cause Wi-Fi connectivity issues, so it's important to check for and install any available software updates for your device. This includes updates for your device's operating system, Wi-Fi drivers, and any relevant apps.

Try Connecting to a Different Network: If you're still having trouble connecting to your Wi-Fi network, try connecting to a different Wi-Fi network to see if the issue is specific to your network or to your device. My favorite testing ground is Starbucks, because they're close and their network is pretty easy to connect to. If you can't get it to connect to Starbucks, you definitely have a problem.

Contact Tech Support: Get the make and model of your Router, if it's separate from your Modem. Have your computer operating system information handy, too. Make sure you have completed all the above steps, because they're going to ask you. Good luck!

Crashing Apps

Apps may crash because of outdated software, conflicting apps, or corrupt files.

Update Your Apps: Outdated software can cause app crashes, so it's important to check for and install any available updates for your apps. This includes updates for both the app itself and for your device's operating system.

Clear App Cache: Sometimes app crashes can be caused by corrupted cache data. What is cache data? It's all the stuff left behind in your computer after you finish using an app or website. It includes cookies and other data bits. Websites store this information on your hard drive so you can use their site more quickly next time, without them needing to download things again. After a while, that cache data and temporary files and folders can pile up, just like junk mail on your counter. To clear the cache, go to your device's settings (sometimes found by looking for a little gear-like icon), find the app in question, and select "Clear Cache" or "Clear Data."

Uninstall and Reinstall the App: If clearing the cache doesn't resolve the issue, try uninstalling and then reinstalling the app. This can help ensure that you're using the most up-to-date version of the app, and can also help clear any underlying issues that may be causing the app to crash.

Check for Conflicting Apps: Sometimes conflicts between apps can cause crashes. If you've recently installed a new app and are experiencing crashes, try uninstalling that app and rebooting to see if it resolves the issue. Also, search online for "*App A* conflicts" where *App A* is your problem child, and see what comes out.

Check for Corrupt Files: Corrupt files can

also cause app crashes. Try deleting any temporary files or downloaded files that may be corrupt and see if that resolves the issue.

Reboot Your Device: Yes, tech support's favorite answer - because it almost always works! Try Restart first, test the app, then if that doesn't fix it, try Power Off and test again.

Seek Professional Help: If you've tried all of these troubleshooting tips and are still experiencing app crashes, you may need to seek professional help (and I don't mean the psychiatric kind, although it may feel like it by now!). Contact the app's developer or your device's tech support team for assistance.

CHAPTER 13

Final Words to the Wise

Congratulations, you have made it to the final chapter! Over the course of this book, I have covered everything from keeping your cool and cultivating your curiosity to enhancing your productivity to saving money by avoiding unnecessary tech, and even dipping into the rough waters of troubleshooting. And of course, I couldn't forget about the importance of backups and cybersecurity, as well as looking fabulous on screen.

The last part of the book is really just a link to another webpage. I considered creating a resource page for the book, but resources were changing even as I was creating the book! Rather than being obsolete before I published, I created a page that I can keep up to date more easily!

Remember to stay curious and let tech help you do more of what you love to do!

RESOURCE GUIDE

Scan the QR code by pointing your phone at the picture below, or go to the page to get all the links:

https://tech-timid.com

It's a separate page so I can update it more easily, and even add to it when I can find new cool tech! (By the way, it's an example of a kind of landing page, from Chapter 9!)

Note: A few of the links are affiliate links, so I may get compensated for any purchase that you make. If you're not an affiliate of anyone or any product, you might be missing out on a great business opportunity that takes very little effort for a lot of payback. Don't be like me - start now!

Do you have more tech questions?

You can get a complimentary 45-minute review of your business tech by going to:

http://mstechcoach.com

or by scanning the QR code below:

ABOUT THE AUTHOR

Sue Wilhite is an experienced business consultant, coach, and speaker with over 25 years of experience in the personal and professional development field. She is known for her expertise in helping individuals and organizations achieve their goals through her unique approach to strategic planning, leadership development, and personal empowerment.

Sue lives with her wife in the beautiful Sonoma County of California, where she continues to be allergic to both alcohol and marijuana; she had to find different paths to alternate states of consciousness. She currently has 2 dogs, and is waiting to be adopted again by one or more cats.

This page intentionally left blank

Feel free to draw silly pictures or write notes here